Contents

Written by
Alison Hawes

Illustrated by
Ollie Cuthbertson

Series editor **Dee Reid**

T0352005

ALWAYS LEARNING   **PEARSON**

Before reading Haldor and the Drawg

Characters

Haldor

A slave boy

Larvig

A slave girl

New vocabulary

ch1	p3	prow
ch1	p3	calm
ch1	p4	looted

ch2	p11	morphed
ch4	p17	mighty
ch4	p20	homeland

Introduction

Haldor and his friend, Larvig, are sailing home after a raid. Their ship is full of looted gold and slaves. Suddenly, a thick sea mist comes down. Haldor fears that the mist hides an evil drawg – one of the undead who sail the seas in their half ships looking for victims.

Haldor and the **Drawg**

Chapter One

Haldor put his hand on the prow of his ship and looked out to sea. The sky was blue and the sea was calm. Haldor had been away for weeks and now he was pleased to see the snow-covered mountains of home in the distance.

 "This has been a good trip," Haldor grinned. "I am coming home with my ship full of slaves and all the gold and silver I have looted. But I'll be glad to sleep on land again tonight. Won't you?" he said to his friend Larvig. But suddenly the blue sky went dark. In the bottom of the boat, a frightened young slave girl clung to her older brother.

Then, just as suddenly, a thick sea mist came down. Haldor could not see or hear anything. Then he heard the sound of a ship close by. He heard its sail creaking in the wind and the sound of the oars as they dipped in the sea. But he could see nothing.

Haldor's heart began to beat faster.

"You know what this is, don't you?" said Larvig.

Haldor nodded. Then, through the mist, they saw
what they had feared. A half ship was sailing
beside them and at the prow was a drawg.
The young slave girl began to cry.

Chapter Two

The sea mist came down again and the half ship disappeared.

"We must try to out-row the drawg," Haldor yelled. "It's our only chance. Everyone, row for your lives!"

But then they heard a splash and the sound
of wet feet on wood as the drawg jumped on
to the ship. The smell of death filled the air.

Quick as a flash, the drawg grabbed the slave girl
and her brother from the bottom of the boat.
Haldor drew his sword and ran at the drawg.
But he was too late to save the young man. The
drawg had already crushed the life out of him.

Haldor snatched the girl back from the grip of the drawg. Then he sank his sword deep into the drawg's neck.

But the sword snapped as it hit bone. Half of it was sticking out of the drawg's neck. The drawg gave Haldor an evil look.

Then the drawg morphed into a seal and slipped back into the water, taking the dead young man with him. The young girl screamed and hid her face in Haldor's jacket.

"Don't be afraid!" Haldor said to the girl. "I will look after you. I promise."

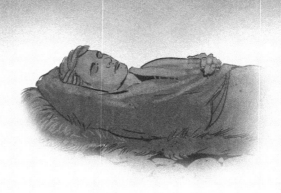

Chapter Three

That night, Haldor and Larvig slept on land for the first time in weeks. But Haldor's dreams were filled with the sight of the drawg and the girl's brother as he sank below the waves.

Then, in the middle of the night, Haldor woke up.
Someone or something was crying. He looked
across at the young slave girl over by the fire. The
girl was awake but she was not crying.

Then a black cat walked out of the shadows.

"It was the cat that was crying!" Haldor

whispered to the girl. The cat walked up to him

and rubbed the back of his hand. Haldor smiled.

The girl smiled too. She held out her hand

towards the cat.

Haldor grinned and knelt next to the young girl.

"Here," he whispered, "I don't know where this cat

is from, but you can keep it."

The girl smiled at Haldor and began to stroke the

cat. Suddenly, her smile turned to a scream!

Chapter Four

Haldor watched in horror as the cat morphed into the drawg. In a second the drawg had crushed the life out of the girl and he flung her lifeless body against the wall. Haldor's heart filled with rage. He gave a loud yell that woke everyone in the Great Hall. Then he rushed at the drawg.

"I promised I would look after her," Haldor yelled, "and I have failed!"

His anger made him strong and, with a mighty roar, he attacked the drawg. As they fought they rolled across the floor and into the great fire.

The flames hissed as the drawg burned. But Haldor didn't let go until the drawg had turned to ash. Haldor's hands began to burn too but he didn't seem to feel any pain.

"You must throw the ashes into the sea," Larvig said, "or the drawg will return."

"Yes," said Haldor, pushing his friend aside, "but there is something else I must do first."

Then Haldor picked up the girl's body and carried it high up on the cliffs. There he dug a grave for her facing the sea so that, if she were to wake, she would look down at the sea where her brother lay, and look across the sea to her homeland far away.

Quiz

Literal comprehension
p4 What was the first sign that the drawg
was approaching?
p14 What was the second creature the drawg used
as a disguise?
p20 Where does Haldor choose to bury the
girl's body? Why?

Inferential comprehension
p10–11 How can you tell that a drawg cannot
be killed by a sword?
p12 Why were Haldor's dreams troubled?
p14 Why was the drawg clever to morph into a cat?

Personal response
- Would you believe Haldor could look after you if
  you were the slave girl?
- Would you have been tricked by the black cat?
- Would you have fought the drawg after it killed
  the slave girl?

Author's style

p6 How does the author show that Haldor
is anxious?
p8 Which description does the author use to
show that the drawg is one of the undead?
p9 Find two descriptions that show that the
drawg is very strong.

21

Characters

- **Orla** (a slave girl captured by Haldor)
- **Bayen** (Orla's older brother)
- **Haldor** (a brave warrior)
- **Larvig** (Haldor's friend)

Setting the scene

Haldor and his men are sailing home after a successful raid. Their ship is full of slaves and stolen treasure. Suddenly, the sky goes dark and a thick sea mist comes down. Haldor and his men can hear the creaking of sails nearby. They fear something evil is out there in the mist.

Orla: Why has it gone dark in the daytime?

Bayen: Don't be afraid, Orla. It must be a storm coming.

Orla: Where do you think they are taking us?

Bayen: Back to their land.

Orla: What will they do to us?

Bayen: Sssh! I will protect you.

Haldor: What are your names?

Orla: My brother is Bayen and I am Orla.

Haldor: Once I had a sister called Orla.

Orla: What happened to your sister?

Larvig: She drowned. Haldor tried to save her but he couldn't.

Haldor: You are wrong about the storm. This darkness is no storm.

Bayen: But the sky is dark in the daytime. It must be a storm!

Larvig: No. The sea is too calm.

Orla: Then what is making it so dark?

Haldor: There's something evil out there in the mist. I fear it may be a drawg.

Orla: What is a drawg?

Larvig: A drawg is a foul creature. It is the bloated corpse of the walking dead.

Haldor: It sails the seas in its half ship looking for victims.

Orla: We're all going to die!

Haldor: I will protect my ship from this evil creature.

Bayen: Ha! You couldn't save your own sister from drowning! How are you going to save us from a drawg?

Larvig: Be quiet or I will cut out your tongue!

Orla: Sssh! What's that noise?

Bayen: I can't hear anything.

Orla: It might be the drawg coming to get us.

Haldor: The girl is right. There is a ship close by. I can hear the creaking of its sails.

Larvig: And that smell is the foul smell of death. It must be a drawg, just as we feared.

Haldor: We must try to out-row the drawg. Row for your lives!

Larvig: It's too late for that. I can see a dark shape rising out of the mist.

Haldor: The drawg is on the ship!

Larvig: And he has the slaves in his claws.

Bayen: Save us from this foul creature!

Haldor: *(to the drawg)* Feel my sword in your bloated corpse.

Larvig: Orla, grab Haldor's arm.

Orla: You have saved me but the drawg has taken my brother.

Haldor: Forgive me. I could not save him. He is only a slave but I wouldn't wish him to die that way.

Larvig: But you saved the girl!

Haldor: I saved this Orla to make up for the Orla I couldn't save.

Quiz

Text comprehension

p26 How does Bayen taunt Haldor?
p27 How does Haldor know the drawg is close?
p29 Who was the Orla Haldor could not save?

Vocabulary

p23 Find a word meaning 'look after'.
p24 Find a word meaning 'smooth, not rough'.
p25 Find a word meaning 'revolting'.

Before reading VIKING WEAPONS

Find out about

• The weapons used by Viking warriors.

New vocabulary

p31 warriors
p32 raided
p34 armour

p37 tunic
p37 chain mail
p38 decorated

Introduction

Viking warriors from Denmark, Sweden and Norway
sailed to countries such as the UK to steal any riches
they could find. Vikings used weapons such as swords,
battle-axes and spears to fight their enemies.

VIKING WEAPONS

Viking Warriors

Viking warriors were fierce fighters. They were some of the fiercest fighters ever known because they were not afraid to die in battle. Vikings used their ships to fight battles far away.

Raids

Viking warriors from Denmark, Sweden and Norway sailed to countries such as the UK and Ireland. They raided homes and churches and took any riches they could find.

Boys as young as sixteen took part in raids.

Weapons

Swords

A sword was the weapon all Viking warriors wanted. Swords were made of iron or steel, and they were very expensive. Only warriors from rich families could afford them. Some warriors gave their swords names, such as Hole-maker!

Battle-axes

Many Viking warriors fought using an axe with a long handle. This was called a battle-axe. This was a deadly weapon that could cut through the armour of the enemy. Axes were also used as tools. In battle, warriors also carried a knife and a bow and arrows.

Axes were made of iron and had a very sharp edge.

Spears

Viking spears were long and very sharp. They were used in two ways. Some were thrown at the enemy. Some were used in hand-to-hand fighting. Some Viking warriors could throw two spears at once, one from each hand!

Defence

Shields

Viking warriors carried a round wooden shield to protect themselves. These shields could be up to a metre across. The shield protected the warrior's body all the way from his shoulder to the top of his leg. At the back of the shield was a metal plate. This protected the warrior's hand.

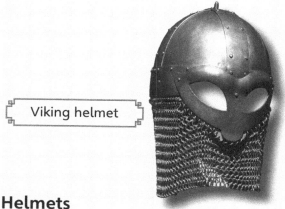

Viking helmet

Helmets

In battle, Vikings wore helmets to protect their heads. The helmets were made of leather or iron. Some of the metal helmets had a strip down the middle to protect the warrior's nose.

Body armour

Some warriors wore a padded leather tunic to protect their body. Some warriors wore a chain mail shirt. These were expensive to make and were only worn by warriors from rich families.

The Vikings decorated their swords and battle-axes and handed them down from father to son. The decorations were a sign of how rich a warrior was.

Weapons were very important to the Vikings. In a battle, an iron sword and a sharp battle-axe could save a warrior's life.

Quiz

Text comprehension

Literal comprehension
p33 Why didn't all warriors have a sword?
p35 How did Viking warriors use spears?
p36 Why did some metal helmets have a strip down the middle?

Inferential comprehension
p32 Why did Vikings raid churches?
p33 Why were swords very expensive?
p38 Why did warriors decorate their swords?

Personal response
- What would you name your sword?
- Why might you prefer to be a rich Viking warrior?
- What would have been your preferred weapon: sword, battle-axe or spear? Why?

Non-fiction features

p34 What is the definition of a battle-axe?
p36 What are the subheadings on this page?
p38 Think of a label for this picture.

Published by Pearson Education Limited, Edinburgh Gate, Harlow, Essex, CM20 2JE.

www.pearsonschoolsandfecolleges.co.uk

Text © Pearson Education Limited 2012

Edited by Jo Dilloway
Designed by Tony Richardson and Siu Hang Wong
Original illustrations © Pearson Education Limited 2012
Illustrated by Ollie Cuthbertson
Cover design by Siu Hang Wong
Picture research by Melissa Allison
Cover illustration © Pearson Education Limited 2012

The right of Alison Hawes to be identified as author of this work has been asserted by her in
accordance with the Copyright, Designs and Patents Act 1988.

First published 2012

24
17

British Library Cataloguing in Publication Data
A catalogue record for this book is available from the British Library

ISBN 978 0 435 07098 4

Acknowledgements
The author and publisher would like to thank the following individuals and organisations for permission
to reproduce photographs:

(Key: b-bottom; c-centre; l-left; r-right; t-top)

Alamy Images: Richard Peel 37; Corbis: Ted Spiegel 38; FotoLibra: Dave Stewart 32, Mandy Collins
34–35; Getty Images: Nordic Photos 31, The Bridgeman Art Library 33; Photolibrary.com: John Coutt
1, 34; SuperStock: age fotostock 36

Cover images: Back: FotoLibra: Dave Stewart

All other images © Pearson Education

Every effort has been made to contact copyright holders of material reproduced in this book. Any
omissions will be rectified in subsequent printings if notice is given to the publishers.